My Hero

Laura Husar Garcia

A Harcourt Achieve Imprint

www.Rigby.com
1-800-531-5015

Sarah is working on a school project about different kinds of jobs.
She has chosen to **interview** her dad because his job is very exciting.
He is a firefighter in Chicago.

Sarah

Dad, what do you and the other firefighters do when the fire **alarm** rings?

fire alarm

Dad

When we hear the fire alarm,
we slide down the pole
into the garage.
Then we put on our suits
and get into our truck
as fast as we can.

Do you wear special clothes when you fight a fire?

Sarah

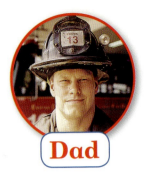

Dad

We have to wear special suits that **protect** us from the fire. The suits are very heavy! We also wear special masks and boots.

mask

helmet

gloves

pants

boots

KOSTED

firefighter mask

Sarah

Is it hard for you to talk while you are wearing your mask?

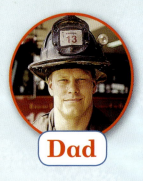

Yes, it's difficult to talk with my mask on. I wear it to protect me from breathing smoke. The mask also helps me see in the smoke.

firefighters training

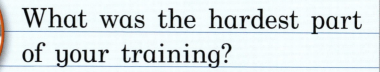

What was the hardest part of your training?

Sarah

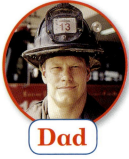

Dad

I had to go through a lot of training to become a firefighter.
The hardest part was climbing up a 100-foot-tall ladder.
I had to practice and practice until I could do it well.

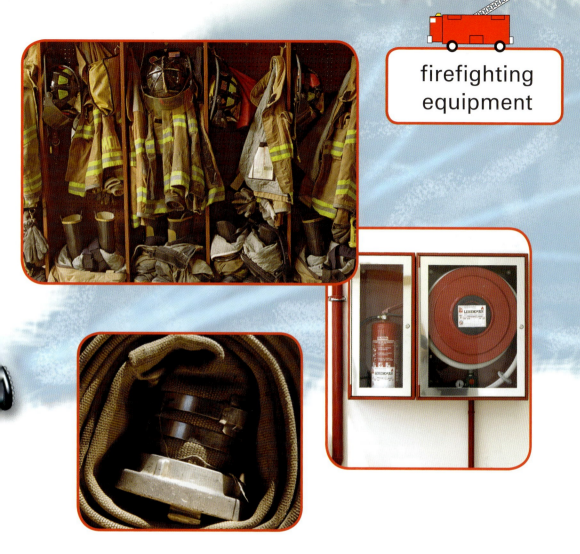

firefighting
equipment

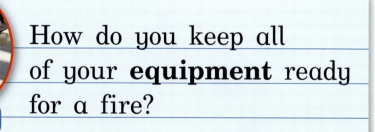

How do you keep all
of your **equipment** ready
for a fire?

Sarah

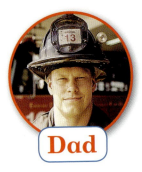

Dad

We keep all of our equipment
clean and ready to use.
The most important equipment
are the hoses.
We test our hoses often
by filling them with water
and checking for **leaks**.

Sarah

What do you and the other firefighters do at the firehouse when there isn't a fire?

Dad

We clean the equipment
and we cook meals.
We also try to have some fun.
We love playing basketball!

Sarah

How do you stay strong for your job?

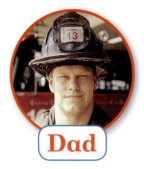

Dad

I exercise a lot. Lifting weights really keeps me strong.

Sarah

Thank you for answering
my questions, Dad.
I am so proud of you!

Glossary

alarm something that makes a noise when there's danger

equipment tools and clothing used for a certain job

interview ask someone questions to get information

leaks cracks or holes in something that let out water or gas

protect keep someone from being hurt